Inspiration for the Heart, Mind, and Soul

From Darkness to Light

INSPIRATIONAL M.L.U

authorHOUSE®

AuthorHouse™
1663 Liberty Drive
Bloomington, IN 47403
www.authorhouse.com
Phone: 1-800-839-8640

First published by AuthorHouse 2/10/2011

ISBN: 978-1-4567-3809-9 (sc)

Printed in the United States of America

Any people depicted in stock imagery provided by Thinkstock are models,
and such images are being used for illustrative purposes only.
Certain stock imagery © Thinkstock.

This book is printed on acid-free paper.

ABOUT THE AUTHOR

Michael was born and raised in Chicago, Illinois and knows the true meaning of adversity. It was through one of his darkest moments that he began to see "the light." This enlightening experience gave him a purpose to help motivate and inspire others to follow their dreams and to always aspire to be the best regardless of their present circumstances. Michael has studied Psychology and has taken part in numerous community service projects. His passion is to share his message that everyone who has a past can convert his or her negative experiences into a positive message for the younger generation one child at a time.

INTRODUCTION

Before one starts this journey, visualize walking in deep snow. You will need extra force to walk through. That's what GOD does for those that willingly come to him. He makes whatever burden or problem one has lighter when it seems to hard to go through. Life is a lesson where one continues to learn. GOD used my life to demonstrate that change for better can and will occur in a person's life. He will take the seemingly impossible and create an avenue for the possible to unfold. This is how he gets the glory. He's the only one that can and will put all the broken pieces together that fell apart. All he wants is a chance. God bless the heart, mind, and soul of the individual(s) that read this book.

TABLE OF CONTENTS

FROM DARKNESS TO LIGHT

Coming from darkness to the light
The path becomes clearer with a new vision and sight
No blinds in the way covering the eyes
Seeing life for what it really is a great surprise
A gift waiting for God's children to come
It was created specifically for his daughters and sons
The ones that have been held back for so long
God will uncover the darkness so you can move on
To a different level and specific place
First you must learn to seek his face
He'll open the door and the sun will shine through so bright
No longer in the darkness because now you can see the light
No longer suppressed because the truth has been unfurled
The truth about God and the ways of this world

MY PRAYER

As I hold this pen in my hand I pray the truth come at demand
To tell of my shortcomings which may be someone
else's too If you put yourself in my shoes I might
relate to you or Maybe someone close at hand
Be still and sensitive to these words the beginning of taking a stand
I've been given a new beginning to help someone else Now the
rest is left to yourself Fear not because you are not alone
I like to call him the big guy sitting on the throne
He opened my eyes and he will do the same for you I
wouldn't tell you if it weren't true So please grab hold and
don't let go God will show you how to take back control.

THIS PLACE (I.A.M)

This was a place of peace with no distractions
Everything was to God's satisfaction
He used this place to give birth to the first man
Setting out to accomplish one goal according to his plan
Everything here was perfect at first
Until man's disobedience made him his own curse
To where everyone after him fell in line
Born with the choice to know the truth or stay blind
Right and wrong is the name of this song
Many can't find right because they listen to the wrong tunes
Wondering why their lives seem so doomed
God's place has been taken and his children left for dead
Greed envy and lust made most of the world turn their heads
Which made many neglect him because they don't have a clue
How would one feel if he did the same too
If it weren't for his son Jesus he wouldn't know you
He opened the door for everyone to come through
So why have many taken his name and given it a big twist
That's why the world of today looks like it don't exist
Deception and trickery has gotten the majority so blind
To where the lives some live they think it's fine
But it's not because the truth is not in your heart
That makes you a liar
The outside may look good but on the inside the soul is on fire

ILLUSTRATION FOR THIS PLACE (I.A.M)

This place was written in reverence to my creator God. He showed me the purpose of this vessel that I make up. This is where his spirit dwells, which was made for his purpose and not mine. It's to give praise to him through all my circumstances and situations. I came to an understanding of the truth. It helped me not to continue to make selfish mistakes, pre-judge, willingly or unwillingly destroy the spirit of others, and not lust for money or power. These will turn a right spirit into a wrong spirit, which will make or keep one blind even though one may see. That's why many commit the offenses they do today because the truth is in them, but not in their heart. The surroundings or material things may seem pleasant, but on the inside the soul is saying differently and it will show. In all I am grateful for who I've become today because I know it's God's purpose. I can now be a blessing or inspiration to others hoping one will come to believe and know him.

Fallen Star

You can be seen from afar but many don't know
who you are and what you are here to do
Make one's life full of torment and misery so they won't have a clue
To what's going on and why things aren't going his or her way
It's because one chooses to obey
Wrong when they think it is right
Not knowing their spirit is dead and don't know how to put up a fight
How can this be one might say I walk and I talk each and every day
So one continues on this path of self-destruction
Money fame and fortune it controls you because
you listened to his instruction
That's his job and what he came to do
Accuse steal and kill so he can keep doubt in you
That's why he's called the fallen star
He himself was just like you
He cherished everything wrong to where his spirit couldn't move
He shows and tells you nothing good ever comes from me
That's why the fallen star hopes you never find me G.O.D
The one who can help you see who you really are and
pull the cover off the wicked one the fallen star

ILLUSTRATION FOR FALLEN STAR

This poem was written to show others of this world, whether one wants to believe it or not what we are up against. If a person is not standing for something he or she will fall for anything. These words are deeper than they appear to be. The darkness in my life was so thick that I literally felt it. This was my life lacking understanding, not knowing why the things I shouldn't have been doing I was and the things I should have been doing I wasn't. Don't focus on the difference, but if there is a similarity. What I mean by this is the outcome of whatever the situation may be. By the time one reads this book some light will be instilled on the inside for change and all one has to do is turn it on. In other words speak it into existence and live it. Convey it the same way one spoke or speaks negativity into existence, which needs to be eliminated. Even where there is light present it can only get brighter and shine for others who are in complete darkness.

Until Death Do Us Apart

A great multitude prepared to go out for battle not knowing
this was a fight where victory wouldn't be theirs
Instead they would become prisoners of the wrong war and
sentenced to death without realizing they were spiritually dead
When they crossed enemy line the trap that was waiting sucked
them in one by one leaving behind loved ones to fend for themselves
All that was left was big void of loneliness and guilt wondering
if they were part of the cause for this self-destruction
that now has them shackled for life or part of it
Now loved ones are forced to attend this negative tour of duty camp
where you can see the pain and misery of all the fallen soldiers there
Which in reality has their infantry soldiers believing that it's ok to
fight this war without realizing the fight is already fixed and there's
no victory in committing crimes or being incarcerated repetitiously
or for the rest of life leaving behind a child husband or wife

ILLUSTRATION FOR UNTIL DEATH DO US APART

The Illustration for Until Death Do Us apart was written for people Who have prepared themselves for battle. Many don't realize what they're actually partaking in won't lead them anywhere but to self-destruction. The fight is no longer that person's, it's now their loved ones standing on the front line too. Even if they are close or miles away from one another, both now have to endure the pain and misery until that day comes. They pray for that day to see each other whole hearted again and no longer chasing to get what's theirs negatively. The fight is fixed and you can't win this one. I have been there. Negativity pays and I guarantee you won't like it. Strive to be positive and I promise you'll appreciate that pay. My life has changed for better and I strive to share my light with others wherever I go.

THOUGHT WAS THE CAUSE

The thought was the cause of it all
That's what made me take that great fall
The mind can be so deceiving
It will make you feel dead inside to where you're grieving
Crying when there's nothing really wrong
All you can do is call on the big guy sitting on the throne
The king may I say who he really is
He's the only one that will handle his biz-ness
Eliminate the real problem we call stress
Which keeps my fellow man or woman so far down
To where you're constantly on the ground
You can get up if you sincerely want to and this is all you have to do
Call on him whether good or bad
He'll show you why he's referred to as dad
He'll never leave nor will he forsake you
He sacrificed his son to show that he's true All the
time what he's trying to say is that he loves you
So rest your mind and thoughts upon his seed
Whom he makes free is free indeed
That's if you only believe

My Mind Is Against Me

My mind is against me or was I against it
That's what I ask myself trying to get out of this pit
This whole I dug for myself
Leave it to those negative thoughts there will be nothing left
What should I do with this mind of mine
Every time I listen to it I end up in a bind
If I'm not locked up for committing a crime
I'm chasing the clock trying to catch back up with time
That I've lost because I listened to those negative
thoughts in my mind my boss
How do I get my mind instead of it getting me
Turn that negative to a positive by finding G.O.D
Free my mind and my soul
Keep running the race and run it bold
It doesn't matter what place I come in
As long as I run it to the end
Crossing the line with my head up high
Those negative thoughts have said good-bye
I'm very grateful I made through
It makes me appreciate myself plus life and so will you

ILLUSTRATION FOR MY MIND IS AGAINST ME AND THE THOUGHT WAS THE CAUSE

I wrote these poems for anyone who wants to know how powerful the mind is. It can be detrimental if used the wrong way. You can end up in a cycle filled with frustration, stress, and guilt. The choices I made all started in my mind or thoughts. These thoughts only I created and obeyed, which had out weighed my positive thoughts. I ended up hanging in the streets, and addicted to drugs. The outcome became repetitious. It consisted of jail and institutions. I believed that drugs were my biggest problem. They turned out to be only a portion of it. I had to find out what played the biggest part to my problem. I found that my greatest set back was my thinking process. Now with this conclusion it was time to work on the solution. I had to renew my mind and build a solid foundation. There are many challenges in this world, but one can overcome them. I had to decipher the differences and similarities for myself with a stronger hand showing me the way. Once this process started, my mind and I started working as one instead of against each another.

SUICIDE MISSION

I committed suicide mission from day to day
Destroying myself in ever single way
By taking chances of doing not what's right
Without realizing I was killing myself without spite
On the inside I was building a bomb
Ready to be set off with the flip of the thumb
Going up like flames from a fire
To hot to control with no desire
Even when I tried to put up a fight
My battle has gotten too strong
The one with the power has lost his might
Power he once had that kept him at peace
Now he finds himself on his knees
Trying to get up from the mission that knocked him down
Before he completely destroys himself
He must find a way to turn it around
Disfigure the negative power that took control
Find a way to renew his soul
Find a way back to the real mission at hand
No longer killing myself learning to take a stand
No longer being suppressed on a day to day basis
I've found someone who knows process of elimination
I've put my faith and trust in him
Me continuing suicide missions became very slim
His precious name is GOD almighty
If you let him he'll take control of your heart mind and soul
The thing we call body

ILLUSTRATION FOR SUICIDE MISSION

I was inspired to write suicide mission because, we as people take on missions from the day we are born. I took on positive missions daily at an adolescent age. By some strange twist of faith I wandered away to negative missions at an early adult age. They were self-destructive and blew up in no time. I strayed away to gangs, drugs, etc. These buried the good spirit inside of me and led me straight to incarceration. In other words without realizing it I had started committing suicide missions from day to day. I was putting my life on the line. I was chasing illusions and the consequences that came along with them. I became a follower instead of the leader that I was created to be. I reaped the benefits of this miserably. I started realizing I had to find a solution to my problem(s) before I explode on the inside. At that point I wouldn't know what to do. It was just a yet, but I thank God myself and others didn't get a chance to find out. I pray daily and dedicate this poem to individuals who are partaking in any deceitful activities. I hope that one finds his or her way back to the positive mission they started, before my yet becomes yours.

EMOTIONS

The innermost being that you're made of
I call darkness and light
To let one know when things are good bad wrong or right
These feelings I thought I could only see and never touch
That's why they lay down until you or someone brings them up
Come to life to show you who you really are
Then you can feel them from afar
Can I handle these emotions or inside feelings
If I don't deal with them the outside will become revealing
That's why I don't judge a book by its cover
The human eye will make it look good like no other
But the inside will show another
So grab hold tie a knot and don't let go
Get to know your emotions and you will start to grow
So you can deal with them instead of them dealing with you
Trust in God and he will teach you along the way too

ILLUSTRATION FOR EMOTIONS

These inside feelings can be very detrimental in a person's life especially if you don't know how or what you're dealing with. They come to life at any given moment in any situation. Anyone can deal with feelings when the moment is good. What about when it's the opposite? I viewed my past and found out that I didn't do a really good job dealing with my emotions. I used drugs and alcohol constantly, but did not understand why. I now understand that I was trying to camouflage my hurt, guilt or whatever it may have been. Discipline is very important. It directs or redirects a person while on his or her path. I've learned a lesson to where my life has taken a turn for better. I am still learning to this day. I realize I can't hide from life or what goes on in life. I'm learning to deal with my feelings and except life on its terms because, sooner or later you will have to deal with your emotions or they will deal with you. That outcome may or may not be pleasing to or for yourself. Don't wait until there are no more chances left. Anything is possible, but you have to deeply believe it.

B.A.S.A.L (Brothers and Sisters and Love)

Why do we commit offenses against one another and call each
other sister or brother
Hurt someone you say you love without a doubt
This is something I've been struggling with trying to figure out
Inflict agony and pain upon oneself and try to blame it on
someone else
Take away from others because you don't have a clue
It was freely given to them and freely given to you
Take responsibility for your own actions
That's the only way to finding satisfaction
Release that negative pressure and let it go
That power inside of you will start to flow
When you dig inside where the sun resides
You'll find yourself no longer by the way side
Then this peace will come out of you as humble as a dove
My brothers and sisters it's called love

ILLUSTRATION FOR B.A.S.A.L
(BROTHERS AND SISTERS AND LOVE)

I was inspired to write this poem for my two sisters that never gave up on their brother. They displayed their concern for me through all of my encounters. I robbed them of a brother and uncle to my nephews. I was headed down destruction and tried to blame everyone, but the right one for my mistakes. This pain I carried had gotten so strong. I continued thinking about the part they played in helping me mature and the wrong turn I took for a vast amount of time. These played a major part in me wanting to change. Once I stayed committed to change that winner on the inside of me started to flourish. They never ceased to encourage me, but I had to find out the hard way. To this day I display that same love back unconditionally and I am very grateful for my sisters. That's the same kind of love God displayed to this world when he sacrificed his son.

Unconditional Love

WHERE ARE YOU

Where are you chosen ones
I look in the places I made but I can't find you
Have you taken a wrong turn to find yourself all alone
Have you wandered away from the place called home
Where are you in places one shouldn't be seen
Hugging street corners like it's the love no one can intervene
Locked behind bars strapped with weapons ready to fight
Wondering if you'll ever make it out by your own might
Strung out on drugs
Drowning in misery looking for a hug
Lost in gangs just to create a false name
Creating dysfunctional families now they're stuck with the blame
Because you left to wander in this wilderness all alone
Wondering if you can stop in your tracks and come back home
You can come back if you desire too
Here's a suggestion on what you can do
Get the man or woman right everything else will fall in place
Take it from me I begged for favor mercy and grace
From God not man because man will leave you where you stand
Where am I
In God's light because he took over all my
battles and struggles we call fights

ILLUSTRATION FOR WHERE ARE YOU

I was inspired to write where are you to keep hope and faith in God within myself. I know I'm not the only person that has or is going through these dilemmas. I strayed away from home where I was under the best supervision anyone can have. I wandered off with the common guys and girls. These may be right there in your family or the environment. Whoever it is if not positive that's where you'll end up, in the streets. Don't mimic what I did and drop out of school, use drugs, and/or end up in some so call gang. I guarantee one if not all of these will definitely happen. The only benefit you'll get is jail, institutions, or death. I witnessed to all of these, even the death because I was spiritually dead. I was blessed not to have experienced the physical death, but came close on numerous occasions. I know God has my best interest. On top of that my family had to witness to me partaking in those negative experiences. They now help me stay afloat and try to mend wounds and seek forgiveness. Forgiveness doesn't come easy when one constantly comes and goes. Now that I've gotten myself together, God will take care of the rest. It will happen if one doesn't give up. I sincerely hope this poem and illustration helps someone at least try to find their way back home where they rightfully belong. Find that place of peace within yourself.

DEATH TO LIFE

Can you tell that I am lost by the way my mind goes in and out
Trying to fool the world without a doubt
I thought I was looking good but I was really looking bad
Couldn't face myself in the mirror so so sad
Who am I really fooling me or you
That's not hard to figure out without a clue
What's going on with me is the question at hand
Son seeking to become a man
Trying to get over what I'm beneath
This drug has taken my soul
I call it thief
It will kill steal and destroy everything you have
Because you chose to come down this lonely path
Path of destruction loneliness and guilt
Tearing down this temple that God has built
No foundation could be what's wrong
With a house made of sand it won't stand strong
Solid rock is what I need and found indeed
No matter what tries to tear it back down it won't succeed
I've cleaned my house and started seeking knowledge
I eliminated my excess baggage known to me as garbage
Now that my life has started coming together
I know I can withstand any kind of stormy weather

ILLUSTRATION FOR DEATH TO LIFE

These poetic verses were written by inspiration from god. I want to show and tell the truth on how my spirit was broken by my own choices and desires. These made my life torment until I found God through Jesus Christ. He lifted my spirit so I can become the man he created me to be and become an inspiration to others who want change. If it happened for me the same can happen for you. We are mere images of one another. Although there may be differences, there are similarities. This situation became the beginning to my trials, errors, and conquers within myself and in society. They actually helped me become a stronger person to where I live to encourage people of all walks of life. It may be you, a loved one, or friend. One will see before it's over with there was only one life we all walked.

The Unseen that's Seen

You can't see me but I'm there
Just believe in me and I'll handle all of your cares
You trusted in things that you could see which did you all wrong
Unlike them I aim to please and make you strong
When you're weak and can't seek help
That's why you need faith
I'll step in and make my presence felt
Change things for better not worse
Eliminate strong holds that many call curse
Which you thought you were under
Why would I hurt you and I sacrificed my younger
Hoping you will give up strife
Become a witness for me to help others find life
Bring them back alive no longer dead on the inside
Because your light has been turned on
Others would know you didn't do it on your own
Now after this I hope they will see the unseen and come to
a standstill so I can intervene

ILLUSTRATION FOR THE UNSEEN THAT'S SEEN

I wrote The Unseen that's Seen in reflection of my own life. I put more trust in all the wrong people, places and things believing these were the solutions to all my problems. This negativity actually made my situations in life worse. One can see from the poems and illustrations I wrote in the beginning, I had my faith and trust in all the wrong places. It wasn't until I surrendered my life and will to Jesus Christ that I saw and felt change happening in my life. I believed he would put the necessary people I need in my life to have a peaceful and prosperous one. In other words when I admitted defeat the desire to do wrong began to cease and to do right came back to life. In all I live willingly to be a light for God with the hopes of drawing others out of their darkness. All one has to do is come to a standstill so a power greater than oneself can take over.

ADDICTED NO LONGER

I once was addicted to bad but now good things
That's why I can shout with joy when I sing
My story started with tears running down my face
Until I found favor mercy and grace
This man seeking to become a son
Realizes his battles are already won
No longer having to fight against myself and this is true
I now know my fight has never been with you
Within me is where my enemy stood
Had me thinking everyone else was up to no good
Walking around staring at the ground
Everytime I looked up all one saw was a frown
This kept me in the dark for so long
Trying to find my way back home
Struggling with nothing but destitution
Once I sobered my mind I started seeing solutions
Which helped me get out of the gutter where I've been so long
That's why I can now say I've moved on
For better not worse
I'm no longer being my own curse

ILLUSTRATION FOR ADDICTED NO LONGER

To be addicted to anything is to create a habit-forming situation. It doesn't occur overnight. It is a repetitious occurrence of events. They will either work for or against you. My addictions started at a young age and continued for over a decade. I was addicted to mind, and mood-altering substances. These substances will take a pure mind, body, and soul into a place where there is plenty of weeping. Everything and everyone will become your enemy when it is actually yourself. Many think our fight is against one another, but it is not. It is against things one can't imagine. They hide deep within our subconscious and can surface at any given moment. Wherever there is a problem, there is a solution. A determined heart with a little belief in a power greater than self will open doors to a new pathway. I became opened-minded to positive information, which helped me become self-aware with a new dignity about myself. Many helped me overcome the obstacles I faced. My goal is to pass the information to the next person that need and wants it.

GOOD-BYE

I'm saying bye to that old man
God has shown me how to take a stand
He helped me until I could stand own my own
Once a baby now I'm becoming grown
Being faithful to my father who opened my eyes
What a great feeling to my surprise
I did everything possible that I could
Until God said taste me and see that I'm good
Not the things I use to do
Which kept me in the dark but now I see the light
No longer having to battle for God said it's his fight
I put my faith and trust in him
Things impossible with man became possible through him
His children are perishing from the lack of knowledge
The wisdom god has for you is greater than any college
He'll take an individual and turn you into a great woman or man
It will happen if one takes a stand
You might stumble or might even fall
Remember God created you
You can knock down the biggest giant
Even if it stands ten feet tall
That's the power god has which he instilled it in you
There's nothing on this earth you can't do
If one wants to make it through
Call on god and he'll guide you too

ILLUSTRATION FOR GOOD-BYE

When I conveyed my message about good-bye, I was specifically talking about my old behaviors. I was desperately searching for answers to explain my thought process, and emotions. A more descriptive form would be why I managed to do the negative things I did. I started attending Psychology classes to assist me on my quest for knowledge. I also acquired hidden knowledge from the best seller called the Bible. This information came at little to nothing at all. All I had to pay was attention. I knocked and the door was opened to a wealth of information that amazed my curiosity. If it weren't for my trials, errors, and conquers someone in need wouldn't receive the message I am conveying. I am still learning to this day, but I can now approach situations in life more wisely and humbled. If I make a mistake, I can dust myself off and keep moving forward. It doesn't take a genius to know something is right. It takes one to know when something is wrong and work towards a solution.

Lost and Found

I've had so much doubt for so long
My season has come to help someone move on
By getting these words across
To anyone who's lost and paying for it at any cost
Have you ever thought about things seeming so bad
Especially when you reflect on something you never had
How can I chase my dream without giving up as hard as it seems
Staying focused is the only way I saw to capture my dream
I got my mind on the right track
Then my life started coming in tact
I was lost without a cause life on pause
Going insane causing my own pain
Blaming everybody else
When all I had to do was dig inside myself
That's where the answer hides no more lonely cries
Now I can hold my head high looking toward the sky
Knowing there's a higher power will become plain to see
That's the true blessing having someone watching over me
I gave him my life and I don't have to think twice
He's to me like a husband and wife
I once was lost but now I'm found
There's nothing greater than coming back around
I once was in the dark but now I see the light
I'm being honest with myself
Now I can sleep at night

ILLUSTRATION FOR LOST AND FOUND

I was inspired to write Lost and Found with admiration to give hope and strength to others. Not only did I write this; I also lived a portion of my life being lost. My path was laid out for me, but I strayed away to the wrong things. I strayed away to drugs, and gangs. This eventually led to multiple incarcerations. My sense of direction, purpose, and self-morality had dissipated without me realizing it. I started searching for the true meaning of God. I then started seeing changes in the areas of need. My evaluation allowed me to surface from under the negative obstacles I was beneath. I didn't happen overnight, but a change came into effect. It took time to get in it and it will take time to get out of it. I am still on course for positive change in spite of circumstances or situations. Let your heart be not discouraged. So the question I pose is can the lost be found? I say yes if one only desires to and admit defeat. Remember that I am a witness to being lost, but now I've found God. I dwell in his light and not the light of this world. I have become a light in this world because mine has been turned on.

PROBLEM AND SOLUTION

I was part of the problem and not the solution
Because my mind was drowned with pollution
With no way out to where I can't even fight
Even though I tried with all my might
Fight what held me back for so long
I've got to find a way to make myself strong
Inside out not outside in
That's where my daily fight and struggle begins
With things I didn't believe but only conceive
Which made me loose my self-esteem
Which was constantly breaking me
So I ask myself why have I forsaken thee
Hurt the one I so love best
Is this happening for a reason or maybe a test
So I can stop being part of the problem but part of the solution
Eliminating all destitution
I fed my spirit so I wouldn't continue to be blind
Not only was my soul cleansed I began renewing my mind
I must admit that I'm amazed this far
Before it's over I'll be touching the stars
The sun shines with you whether you believe it or not
You'll be astonished by the power you've got

ILLUSTRATION FOR PROBLEM AND SOLUTION

Understanding is the key ingredient missing to a problem or solution. It doesn't matter how much wisdom or knowledge one may have. If a person doesn't know why they're doing the irresistible, chances are that you're a mere image of me. These are questions I asked myself seeking to turn my life around. Who is the problem, What happened, when did it start, where did it come from, and why? The biggest question was what's the solution? Whatever I did this problem was right there with me. It was present when I slept, woke up, ate, went out, or came in. As I deeply reflected on these questions, I came to the conclusion that I was the problem. Once I understood that I was the problem, I took the initiative to gain my life back. I started seeking solutions. That's the only way I had a chance of trying to mend wounds that I helped to create. I knew I needed a power greater than myself to overcome in victory. Although he was already there, I thank God I found him. I just needed to turn him on so he could work. I have to admit it feels great. I understand that there are many problems that exist in the world. I strive daily so I won't continue to be part of those problems, but part of the solution. Understanding and willingness holds the key.

A Crying Soul no Longer Crying

For without him I was all alone
Wondering why I do so much wrong instead of right
Keep getting knocked down without a fight
Tossing and turning because I can't keep still
Crying knowing this isn't the way I'm supposed to live
This is what I kept saying to myself
I only heard wrong being deaf
Keeping my ears open trying to hear
If I keep this up I'll soon disappear
For good and not get back
Too blind to see my spirit was under attack
By something I couldn't see
My soul was crying Lord have mercy on me
Help me find a way out
So I can believe in myself without a doubt
Eliminate my wrongs and learn to stand up strong
Like a soldier that gives his best
So when my war is over I'll know I passed the test
I feel relieved lying in the bosom of his chest
That's why my soul stopped crying because God knows best

ILLUSTRATION FOR
A CRYING SOUL NO LONGER CRYING

The soul of an individual is his or her inner being. This is where life roots. Its purpose is to guide and direct your heart and mind. I am referring to your spirit. When one does not know what the soul is composed of, the likelihood of an individual going astray increases tremendously. I knew I was a living soul, but ignorant to the true component it possessed. I put everything but the right substance in my spirit. I indulged in many of the activities under the sun. I was blind and could not see. Many may have wondered in the beginning if I actually couldn't see through human eyes. Those are not the eyes I am talking about. The spirit is what I am referring to. It was given to all by God Almighty. He has a power more powerful than anyone or anything on this earth. He will allow one to see it too. I started feeding my spirit the right substance. That would be the word of God. This is where my comfort, peace, and reality came from to help me stop crying on the inside.

No More Weeping

How do you kill a nation made to be Goddesses and saints
Kill the mind and body which leaves a person blank
Kill the spirit and kill the mind
After experiencing this there's nothing left to do but whine
Now I'm crying but I still walk
No one will listen to me especially when I talk
Trying to get across to let you'll know
You were made to rule from the days of old
Positive not negative is the only way to live life on this earth
Live it each day for what it's worth
Put the weapons of mass destruction down
Turn that smile bottom side up no longer a frown
Open the big book and meditate on the words
Ask forgiveness and knowledge called proverbs
Words of wisdom now you have
It will put you on the narrow road formally called path
No more negatively thinking wrong
When people hear you it will be in comparison to a favorite song
Soothing to the heart mind and soul
It's been instilled in you since the days of old
All you have to do is grab hold and don't let go
Thank God for staying knocking at my door
That's why I don't have to cry anymore

ILLUSTRATION FOR NO MORE WEEPING

Crying was something I did on a constant basis. I engaged in this physically and mentally. When one doesn't understand or know that he or she was made to conquer and not be conquered, the likelihood of success being put on hold increases tremendously. Many turn to drugs, gangs, and alcohol for that confidence. In reality they only destroy one's chance at achieving success. An individual's self-esteem, identity, and self-worth has to be found. History has shown me that many may still be lost. How can these attributes be found? Wherever there's a problem the solution lurks right behind it. My solution started surfacing when I dug into my inner spirit. I engaged in seeking a relationship with the son and heavenly father. He is the author and finisher of my faith on this earth. The winner inside of me started coming to life. I returned back to school seeking a degree in psychology, which in return helped me learn more about myself and others. Anything is possible. One has to stand firm and don't deny guidance. God will always be there waiting to help one get to the next level. I guarantee slowly, but surely those tears will vanish. Delay does not mean denial.

A WAY OUT

A way out I thought I'd never find
Until I started renewing my old mind
Focusing on the positive not negative
It gave me enough hope and strength to want to live
A peaceful prosperous and productive life
No longer looking to chase after strife
Seeking to take back what I rightfully own
It was handed down to me from God on the throne
To the ambitious and righteous one
It makes me feel good to know I'm God's son
Son of the light no longer in the dark
Now I see why I have a big heart
Which has taken a turn for better not worse
I'm no longer being my own curse
Who use to do wrong but now learning to do right
It will happen for you if you put up a good fight
Step out the way and let God take control
He'll cleanse your heart mind and purify your soul

ILLUSTRATION FOR A WAY OUT

When someone has gotten so deep into fictitious ways they've created, can a way out be far fetched? I wrote this poem so someone will believe there is a way out. I lived a respective life under the guidance of my beloved mother until I wanted to stray away from doing right to wrong. I ended up in a pit that I dug for myself. In the course of my great fall a lot of people were hurt emotionally. This can actually be worse than being hurt physically. This pain I was experiencing hurt so bad to where I became determined for change. This feeling gave me hope and strength to live. I know there are better things in this world. When I allowed god into my life, he started guiding me out of situations that I put myself in. My thought process enhanced to a different level. I started viewing life like I did previously before I made that wrong turn. In all I'm back on track and moving forward with Jesus Christ leading the way.

FORGIVE ME

Forgive me lord for my wrongs of the past
On my knees seeking forgiveness
Because your love forever lasts
Not worrying about you throwing it back in my face
For you are full of favor mercy and grace
That's why I don't condemn what others do
You're the only judge always faithful and true
Forgiving me for the things that I've done
You told me not to worry my son
Because you're my friend and father
You created me that's why you're called the author
The finisher of my faith
You separated me from others to give me my space
So you can work with me on a one on one basis
To shape and mold me in all the right places
So I can do a job and when it's done
I'll know I've been forgiven because I'm your son

ILLUSTRATION FOR FORGIVE ME

What does it really mean when a person asks for forgiveness? Does it mean that a person did something wrong and wants to correct his or her mistake? Where does forgiveness come from? By any chance does it come from the heart? If an individual can relate to these questions sincerely, chances are that God has or is trying to shape and mold you. All parties have to be willing participants. Forgiveness is an authentic word, but can be misconstrued. This is because of the hidden agenda residing in an individual. It is called bitterness. I stored a lot of bitterness within myself for years. I used all types of excuses and destructive substances to camouflage my hurt, guilt, and shame. I was only destroying myself more and more. I experienced this for a vast amount of time. I woke up three years ago and said enough is enough. I was powerless. I took my wounds to God/Jesus and the healing process began. If anyone I can trust to sincerely forgive me is God. He will not throw my faults back at me any day, month, or years from now. Forgiveness is a small word, but it has a big meaning. It is hard to do in a carnal state of mind. It has to come from the heart. Knowing what it means doesn't make it happen. Forgiveness can be established. It may take time, but at least the process has been put into affect. It will open the door for a true relationship with God and others.

GOD UNDERSTANDS

God understood me when no one else could
Helping me see the things that I shouldn't be doing but should
He gave me his heart when I was falling apart
Shedding his light for a way to see out of the dark
He took the time to stay by my side
Never once his love did he try to hide
God understands that I am not a perfect man
Constantly searching for his purpose and plan
Trying to find the right way to go day by day
Without giving up no matter what anyone has to say
He'll take the pieces that fell apart
Put them back together mending your heart
His love is so strong you can feel it coming through
That's what makes him different from me and you
God is the only one who never complains or has big demands
I love him because he's simple and he understands

ILLUSTRATION FOR GOD UNDERSTANDS

Who best understands an individual walking on the face of this earth? In all my seeking to attain knowledge I left out the main ingredient. That would be an understanding. Can one imagine searching for something with blinds covering his or her eyes? I had no idea that I was walking in darkness. I could see through the human eyes, but I still was blind. I ran into a brick wall on numerous occasions. After experiencing these headaches, the only remedy for my situations was to seek a solution. The only solution I heard of and affordable was God. I actually didn't have to pay him anything, but attention. It became obvious that he was by my side because I'm here sharing my story with others. Once I confessed my belief in him and his son Jesus, those blinds started falling from my eyes. My wrongs became rights because I chose to give him my struggles that many call fights. In spite of the darkness that exists on earth, I'm still striving to help fulfill God's plan.

THE FATHER IN ME

The death of a nation was already proclaimed
No matter what race creed or color it still remains
It wasn't handed down just to me
This was done before existence came to be seen
Not with the eyes which can be an art
With the inner being that plays the major part
The spirit my friend is what I'm talking about
It controls your mind emotions and your heart
These came from the father who gave us our start
Once you get to know him you'll see that he's true
He did it for me and he'll do it for you
Look at my history and you'll see it's true
Get to know him like he knows you
He'll show you on this earth what to do
Definitely not hate or judge one another
Just because the skin is of another color
There are many colors and it's plain to see
When it boils down I'm part of you and your part of me
So the real question to one's soul is
Do I know God like God knows me

ILLUSTRATION FOR FATHER IN ME

I was inspired to write father in Me to keep myself strong and with the hopes of giving someone an understanding. When many here the word death they may think of the physical death. That's not the one I've conveyed my message about. I am talking in reference to the spiritual aspect of people. It exist whether one wants to believe it or not. This is the death that many are currently sleeping from. It's the main reason why I indulged in a vast amount of negativity. When I was spiritually dead I became a follower of the wrong things. I was mislead by the blind on numerous occasions. It happened because I was blind myself. I couldn't see what I was getting myself into. Another source was needed to help me understand life and why we do what we do. When I came to God, I came to the understanding that there are many weapons surfacing the face of this earth. Its intentions are to destroy one's self-esteem, self-worth, and identity. If one doesn't know what they're facing, there's a strong likelihood of falling victim. Then you have repeated cycles. This only exists because many don't truthfully know what they're facing. One can get up, but needs to now why he or she keeps falling. I have established a personal relationship with God and he did the same. I have to stay in a position for him to continue working with me and guide me through. I know today and want others to know that our fight is not against one another. It is against things we can't see, but they can be seen through the things we do.

CHIP AWAY

God chips away at a heart made of stone
Resentment and anger changes the right tone
The message God is trying and wants to convey
Because the roadblock has gotten in the way
Making it difficult when he's trying to get through
The message bounces back when it's related to you
What must be done so an understanding can find its place
Keep chipping at the heart until that stone has gone away
Making a path to remove resentment envy anger and doubt
The sun can now shine from within presenting a new route
Days months or even years may pass by
The message will become clearer
Because you will see it through the spiritual eye
The eye that can't be seen but holds the truth
The gift is free only if one converts back as a youth
Full of faith knowing things will come to pass
Believing in the Alpha and Omega the first and last

CHOSEN ONE

I need someone to take this mission
One who believes nothing about superstition
Someone who will stand up strong
Like a newborn baby standing on his or her own
For the first time to face the encounters in this life
Without giving up like a soldier in a fight
Bringing the honor and glory back home
When a lost soul stops trying to do wrong
But instead starts doing right
It might seem long to you but to me it's like overnight
My chosen one will have characteristics just like me
If you don't know I go by the name of G.O.D
My chosen one won't steer you wrong
His or her job is to help you find your way back home
From the journey where you made the wrong turn
Now it's time to be still look listen and learn
Hear what the still voice is relating to you
If you are obedient it will guide you through
Back to the place where you belong
The place of peace just like home
Then you'll realize you were never alone
Now you can help others like someone helped you
Then you'll realize I father GOD chose you too.

Illustration for Chosen One

Humiliation will build up a person's character. The encounters I've faced previously in life had gotten the best of me. It was only my fault because they were self-inflicted. The lack of understanding and self-willed served its purpose by showing me the cause to my destruction. This turned into humbleness and allowed me to turn my will over to GOD. I soon started taking a stand for myself. I was now ready to re-face life and its encounters again. I've learned to except and deal with my emotions that reside within me. An understanding helped me uncover my wrongs instead of burying them. I've been given a new chance to run on the right track. It took years, but to God it's like overnight. I wouldn't wish my past on my worst enemy. I came to know him as myself. To this day I live to encourage people and let them know about my past, but see me for my present and future. I hope this message helps someone change something in his or her life for the better. I'm still striving because I have the willingness and desire. Someone is helping me along my course. Therefore, it is only right that I help someone who needs and wants it. In return you can give it to someone like it is given to you. Before one knows it, he or she will realize that they were chosen too.

I AM

I'm compared to the one greater than I am
I come from the seed known in the Bible as Ham
I'm blessed and can conquer anything that I do
If you know your history you will know it too
Positive not negative is what I strive to do more and more
I ask Jesus to enter my heart known as the door
The truth internally has made me free
I refuse to let anyone take that away from me
I own it today and so do you
No longer looking to do the wrong I use too
Looking to do what makes me a success
Learning about myself bringing out the best
The conqueror my father said I am
One step at a time in total command
No longer suppressed because I have taken a stand
That's why I'm compared to the great I AM

ILLUSTRATION FOR I AM

Knowing who I am and what my genetic factors consist of was a lesson in the making. I have journeyed in this wilderness for over forty years. Along this course I encountered many shortcomings. I fell on numerous occasions, but I did not stay down. A change of heart brought about a change of mind. This only surfaced believing that there was a power greater than myself. Trying to figure out about the evolving of humanity can be a perplex situation. Many will become lost searching for a clue. The answer lurks where an individual least expects it to be. I took the initiative to research my history. I started my quest within the Bible. There is a wealth of wisdom and knowledge that awaits anyone who seeks it. In all the information that one attains, an understanding is the main ingredient. This information can be incorporated to help one perceive life for what it is worth. I prayed without ceasing for God to show me what was required of me to see. I found out how much favor God has given me and I want to use it in a positive way.

CHANGE

What is change to do better or worse?
To climb that ladder or be your own curse
What is change
Not that which rattles in your pocket
But taking off just like a rocket
Taking off to new expectations
Leaving behind all lamentations
Which kept me crying day and night
Like a newborn baby struggling trying to fight
Trying to walk and talk day and night
I need change with a new beginning
The fight I fought I wasn't winning
Like a roller coaster going up and around
The ride I was on I'm glad it slowed down
Came to a complete stop
Instead of being on the bottom I ended up on top
The highest point I could go where is that I don't know
I'll never know if I don't stay strong
Come face to face with all my wrongs
I'll keep my head up and don't look back
It's called growing up and that's a fact
Growing up is part of change too
I like that feeling how about you
There's nothing constant but to change
If not positive you'll stay the same
So Change for better not worst
Don't end up being your own curse

Illustration for Change

I was inspired to write change with the hopes of shedding light down dark paths. There comes a time and point in every person's life when a critical decision has to be made. I call it change. Change is inevitable in a person's life. It will happen whether one wants it to happen or not. It will be either for better or worse. I had to view my life and the changes that were happening. They were negative changes in the beginning with plenty of misery behind them. This journey continued to progress for years. I never imagined a simple word would turn my life in a new direction. That word is defeat. When I admitted defeat change for better started occurring in my life. I started accepting myself for who I am and the many mistakes that I made. I realize change doesn't happen overnight, but it can start at any given moment. I have accepted change towards being a better individual and a shining light wherever I go.

HEART'S DESIRE

To have a desire burning in your heart
Day after day creates a new and bigger spark
Bringing what use to be in the dark to the light
Setting out to accomplish the impossible and bring it to sight
To show the unthinkable can be done
One after one your blessings will come
Just keep a heart full of fire yes a burning desire
So you can be a light for those that can't see
Things that seem impossible are possible if you only believe
Along with a burning desire to succeed
Put your faith and trust in God
The one whose thoughts and ways are always higher
He'll show you the way to your heart's desire

ILLUSTRATION FOR HEART'S DESIRE

I was inspired to write Heart's desire to show that desires can shape and mold a person's heart. My desires were conceived through my seeing and hearing, which allowed me the choice to pursue or not pursue. Desires come in all shapes, colors, forms and fashions. I chased wrong for a while because of my own ill will, which became poor decision- making. If a mind is cluttered it increases the likelihood of pursuing wrong. Many fall under the deception of believing it to be right. An individual will pursue whatever is implanted in their heart. God will free a person's mind and soul if one allows it to happen. The only way for him to intervene is to humble yourself. Whatever message is transferred to the heart one will start believing it. There are positive and negative influences in this world for a person to consider. Let it be the right one. You will start seeing godly desires. Whatever one continues to think, It will start becoming part of you. Whatever one starts to become they will live. This process has consequences, but it is solely up to the individual in determining which decision he or she will make.

I UNDERSTAND

I understand why some choose to say can't instead of can
This was a word I once used being a man
Knowing the hand I got dealt was all so wrong
But I played the cards to that song
To words I didn't understand that made me feel less of a man
With no plan until I learned to take a stand
For myself through God because he knows best
So I can put that negative can't word to rest
To sleep for good where it belongs
Because I was made to be powerful and strong
To be or do whatever I positively choose
To share with others my inspiration called good news
News for any boy girl women or man
Instead of saying I can't know that you can

ILLUSTRATION FOR I UNDERSTAND

Using the word can't is more crucial than it seems. I was accustomed to bringing life to this word. The fear of doubt incorporated itself into my life. I became afraid of how I would look or what others will say if gave a wrong answer. I felt the same way about making a bad decision. I eventually shut myself off from others and my true character. In other words the belief that I can't came into existence. I allowed my self-esteem to be torn down before I had a chance to build it up. The lack of understanding played a major part towards my self-destruction. I wouldn't have a clue if it weren't for the positive influences and God in my life. I would probably be in one of those negative places I once resided in. I have taken a stand so I won't fall for everything someone throws my way. These are the reason I understand, but don't let my old excuses become part of you. You were created to be power and strong. You can accomplish whatever you set your heart and mind on. Always know that you can and continue to believe it.

LOVE

Love has neither color nor a specific name
Love is not that of riches fortune and fame
Love has a passion that can't be explained
Like the word of God when it's all over it will still remain
In its place waiting to be embraced with arms open wide
Love makes itself known never trying to hide
From the truth of what it really is and what it does
So when you get a chance to meet this love
It will tell you I am as I am just because

ILLUSTRATION FOR LOVE

When I think of love, I think of sacrifice, unconditional, and forgiving. These attributes remind me of God sacrificing his son for the world. He stepped outside of himself to give people a chance at life. Regardless of right and wrong, individuals are given the opportunity to learn the truth about love. Love doesn't consist of what a person has, the color, or the status of a person. Love is as simple as one, two, and three. It goes deeper than the human eye can conceive. Sometimes this word can get misconstrued, but there is always the possibility of turning it around the right way. The flesh of a person can be weak, but the spirit is always willing. I truly hope this message reaches the heart of each and every person that reads this.

MY LOVE

The one whose vessel God used for his purpose to bring forth life
The one who stayed close to me like a man married to his wife
She sacrificed daily from the heart
Did everything she could to stop anything from bringing us apart
The one who helped train me up in the way to go
Taught me things that I should know
The one who stayed true to me when I made a wrong turn
She taught me a lesson so I could learn
The one whose place that could never be taken
She never left nor did she forsake me
The one who stayed true to herself and God
Told me not to take what's easy and make it real hard
The one I'm proud of has a spirit as humble as a dove
I see why she's full of love
My love I'm talking about was the first to hold me in her arms
I love and thank God for her yes my mom

ILLUSTRATION FOR MY LOVE

I was inspired to write My Love because of my mother. She bestowed her love to myself and others all of her life. She never complained or let her adversities interfere with the character she possessed. She planted all the necessary seeds in my spirit. I couldn't administer to them because of the perplexed situations I was facing. She continued to water them faithfully and God brought them to life. I started to become the man she and God knew I was created to be. So I dedicate these life-giving words to my mom and all the mothers of this world. I know at some point adversity tries to creep its way in. Continue to stay strong women and God Bless you all.

A Child's Song

A child's song is soft with harmony and peace
Like trees planted by moving waters with no worries at ease
Just wanting a path and guidance to keep them on course
Bringing joy to everyone that sees and hears their voice
Captivating hearts with their sweet song
A child's song grows stronger with each day
Like his or her age and height so does their might
With a stronger hand to hold them up
Instilling in them never give up even if you fall
Before you learned to walk you learned to crawl
So when you can stand tall on your own
You can face the whole world singing your song

ILLUSTRATION FOR A CHILD'S SONG

I was inspired to write A Child's Song for the children that didn't get the opportunity to face this world and those that are facing this world. Children are so innocent from the day of conception. They have no idea of what to expect in or out of life. They just want to be nurtured by a strong hand until it's time to adventure in this world. They win hearts with their innocence and bring joy to those that stop and stare. While in the process of making transitions they just want that same strong hand to hold them up. That hand will guide them on their quest and help them learn from mistakes. When they are old enough to stand tall and explore on their own that strong hand will be with them. This time it will be their own facing the world.

MY SON

He's seed of my seed known as my son
Looking for steps to follow one by one
Looking for a path to follow that's right
With two things in common his faith and might
Taking heed to the way things are done
As he grows older he'll decipher them as they come
The ways that will help guide him on his own
Being a cautious follower but now becoming grown
Old enough to make the right choices and decisions
One after one with great precision
So when he looks in the mirror and see himself smile
He'll know the things he's doing is worth his while
Doing his best to do what's right
Able to see the difference between good bad wrong or right
Even when his mistakes are done
He needs my love and support because he's my son

ILLUSTRATION FOR MY SON

I wrote this poem for my sons and for all the sons in this world. A son takes on hidden genes or traits bestowed to him. These subconscious attributes play a role in shaping and molding him into who he becomes. This is the biological side of a person. Then you have the journey one must travel toward his destination. Along the way are many influences, which can be either positive or negative. These influences reside within the family, and environment. They also play a major part in helping his characteristics form. An individual can root from the best parenting and fall short. The best solution is to help him understand the mistake and the lesson behind it. This way as he gets older he can have an advantage in deciphering them on his own. Willingness and desire holds the key.

A Daughter's love

The queen I helped to be conceived gives me peace with her smile
That brightens my world every time I think about her
She warms my day even though we're far from one another
My love for her is like my sisters to their brother
She helps me stay on track just thinking about her smile
Whether she believes it or not it's worth my while
She keeps me going so I can help fulfill her dream
To show the world a daughter and father can be a team
Not allowing our opponents to steal the ball
Even though times haven't been the greatest of all
Her love and smile keeps me coming back
Even though I'm addicted I choose not to be set back
Nor keep getting set apart
So we both stay where we belong
In our rightful place each other's heart

Illustration for A daughter's Love

I was truly inspired to write A Daughter's Love because her love is very special to me. I sit back daily and reminisce on the days we've shared together. Trying to display love and being taken away at the same time is an unbearable feeling. I drifted away to the wrong people, places and things. I ended up in all the wrong places one shouldn't be. The streets opened the door to a lot of mischief. My self-esteem and morals vanished into thin air. My life soon became very unstable. I was hurting tremendously, but didn't know how to confide in anyone. I did what I thought I knew best. I resorted to substances to ease the pain. All that did was make my situation worse. I thought I was hurting. I can imagine how my baby girl was feeling. All of this anguish turned into determination for change. I've cleaned my house and added positive information. My love never left, I just had to find a way to love myself again. In all fathers or mothers never mean or intend to hurt their loved ones, but it happens. That hurt can be turned into real love, but forgiveness holds the key. If it's prolonged the likelihood of pain walking in increases tremendously. The best solution is to establish an open communication line with one another. Therefore, one can release any feelings that may interfere with making progress in life.

KING

A king I am yes by far
I come from the seed of the rising star
The one who gets all the glory and remains the same
Just like him people will view me for my good name
Not the things that I have
They'll disappear if I take the wrong path
I'm on the right course and I have a positive voice
Only because I chose to make the right choice
To live humbled with God's favor mercy and grace
One step at a time with him setting the pace
Bringing me to a point where I'm back in control
Restoring what was taken from the days of old
Knowing I can be but I wish not to be alone
Every king should have a queen next to him on his throne

MY QUEEN

My queen is made with the essence of beauty outside and inside out
She know where she's from and going without a doubt
My queen knows how to treat me and I know how to treat her
We're two of a kind like diamond and pearl
My queen has self-esteem built on a solid foundation
I'm to her like she's to me a positive motivation
My queen knows she is blessed
Not because she wears a short short dress
Which leaves no room for any distress
Because her heart and mind is full of ambition
Not worried about any competition
Trying to take away what she rightfully owns
God also made you to sit on a throne
To be treated in the most respectful way
That's why you're called a queen to this day
If you're the queen I'm talking about
Thank God almighty you have no doubt

ILLUSTRATION FOR MY QUEEN

I was inspired to write My Queen for the self-less ladies who played a major part in my life. They displayed how strong and ambitious they were through difficult times. They stood on their own with the same common denominator. That was faith in God. Every hurdle that appeared before them was jumped. It didn't matter how long or high the challenge; they excelled every step of the way without giving up. This taught me the true essence of a lady. So I dedicate this heart-felt poem to all the ladies of this world. You're a queen in God's sight and you should be treated according to the queen that you are. There is nothing more precious and genuine than one of the gifts from God. I call her my Queen.

LITTLE QUEEN

I'm small in stature but I have big dreams
When people see me they call me little queen
I walk tall and I'm not alone
When I grow up I'll know where I belong
Sitting in my own place on my throne
Seeking to achieve whatever I plan
I won't believe in can't I'll know that I can
Because I've been led by a stronger hand
One step at a time learning to take a stand
Bringing out the best that reside in me
Showing the world why I'm called little queen
That's the confidence that I have
Now you see why I am as I am

Little Queen

KING AND QUEEN

A king and queen we are
We both come from the seed of the rising star
The one who gets all the glory and stays the same
Just like him people view us for our good name
Not the things that we have
They will disappear if we take the wrong path
We're both on the right course and have a positive voice
Only because we chose to make the right choice
Sitting on high at the highest altitude
Consoling one another for the perfect mood
So when it's time to come down
We'll be standing next to each other bearing our crowns
Crowns of glory the whole world will see
I'm part of you and you're part of me
That's why God calls us king and queen
The two of us can accomplish anything

SHE UNDERSTANDS

She understood me when no one else could
Helping me see things I shouldn't be doing but should
She gave me her heart when I was falling apart
Being a light for me to find my way out of the dark
She took the time to stay by my side
Never once her love did she try to hide
She understands that I'm a simple man constantly
searching for my purpose and plan
Trying to find my way day by day
Without giving up no matter what anyone has to say
She runs her race at a totally different pace
But she's full of favor mercy and grace
She never complains or has big demands
I love her because she's a simple woman and she understands

QUEEN

I'm made with the essence of beauty outside and inside out
I know where I'm from and where I'm going without a doubt
I know how to treat my king and he knows how to treat me
The two of us will make a perfect team
I have self-esteem built on a solid foundation
I'll be to him like he'll be to me a positive motivation
I know that I'm blessed not because I wear a short short dress
There's no room left for any distress
Because my heart and mind is full of ambition
Not worried about any competition
Trying to take away what I rightfully own
God made me to sit on a throne
To be treated in the most respectful way
That's why I'm called a queen to this day
I know I'm the queen you're talking about
I thank God Almighty I have no doubt

ONE PEOPLE

Yes we can as a nation sitting in the palms of God's hands
Waiting on the people to take a stand
To put together the pieces that fell apart
America looking for a brand new start
Seeking to heal wounds that made many feel doomed
Praying for a remedy to come soon
Even though the medicine people were looking for
God put into work many years ago
He released his angels so it won't stay the same
Correction has come to ease the pain
Giving us all a reason to proclaim
We're a great people and nation all created the same

Illustration for One People

God created a multicultural world for his purpose and plan. When an individual or individuals take a designed blueprint and redesign it without consent, things can and will go wrong. Once it is rebuilt it no longer stands on a solid foundation. One may think it is, but it isn't. In due time the structure starts falling apart because there is no support. I visualize America and the rest of the world facing the same challenge. Many can see that America has encountered problems that did not occur overnight. This dilemma has the likelihood of sending panic throughout the population. Where does this situation stem from? There may be different views of opinions expressed. The real answer roots from a whole instead of one or two. There have been many inspiring individuals sent to convey a message of truth, hope, peace, and prosperity. Individuals have to see it for what it's worth and lean not on thy own understanding. Once perceptions change toward a positive direction, that solid foundation will start strengthening itself. God will show one what his intentions are. Then one can start seeing the true foundation that America actually stands on.

TIME

I stand still for no one or no thing
I keep moving like rivers flowing up stream
People chase me trying to capture their dream
I move slowly but I'll pass by fast
If you miss a beat I'll have control of your first and last
For you choosing to pursue the wrong path
Re-enacting moments like they just gave birth
I advise one to cherish them for what they're worth
You try your best to keep up with me
Just reflect on your life and you will see
I'm gone further before you get a chance to proceed
Now you know it's impossible to keep up with my speed
Chase after your goal or dream
It's more realistically to capture it instead of me
So I'll advise one to do what's best for you
I'll continue to be me

Time

ILLUSTRATION FOR TIME

Time is of the essence. If it isn't managed appropriately, it will slip away from an individual. One will find his or herself trying to catch back up with it. Regardless of the circumstance or situation, it is gone. Nothing is promised to be easy on this journey one takes. I choose to live wise, humbled, but with an understanding. I allowed a vast amount of time to disappear from me. I pursued the wrong things. I was lacking knowledge and an understanding. Although many excuses surfaced, no one else was to blame. I had to learn that time is very precious and I'm only granted a certain amount of it. Once an individual acknowledges that he or she has a purpose, time will be appreciated. This time comes from god. When the clock stops individuals will be held accountable for their time spent. If one is pursuing right, chances are that he or she understands time. If it is vice-versa one may want to pursue right. It can be accomplished and incorporated into ones life. There are many that can attest to this. I am one of them.

WHY

Why does wrong insist on showing up when you're doing right
Continue to keep calling day and night
Talking about things of the past
Using every excuse trying to make you feel bad
Why does wrong try to sound so good
Word after word all you hear is use to or should
Why doesn't wrong care when you've been blessed
with someone special in your life
Who dares to cherish God children husband or wife
Wrong tries to tear down what God builds up
Trying its best to make what's good corrupt
Wrong doesn't admit the role being played is to deceive you
To where you're stuck in life without a clue
Who is this wrong and why won't it go away
Nothing positive does it have to say
Maybe it's the past where there was a lot of wrong
Trying to see if you are who you say you are standing up strong
The next time wrong calls I won't give it the satisfaction
I don't need that negative energy in my life called distraction

ILLUSTRATION FOR WHY

I was inspired to write why to give clarity to anyone who need and wants it. I want to inform individuals that you're not alone in wondering why life's circumstances or situations have taken its toll. There may be differences, but similarities are definitely there. They consist of right, wrong, good, bad, or whatever one wishes to call it. This is my illustration behind Why. When change for better started occurring in my life, I had to clean house. I am referring to the negative people, places, and things that influenced my judgement. I allowed these to hinder me from prospering and becoming a success. I couldn't see the king that God created me to be. I gave my authority away without realizing the detriment I was doing to myself. These wrongs didn't disappear overnight. They continued to remind me of the negative instead of the positive. This was to see if I would fall back into my self- destruction. Wrong doesn't discriminate. It insists on tearing down a foundation, but only if one allows it to happen. My circle today is small and I'm very cautious about who I allow to come in it.

I'm not Alone

Guide me to a place of peace
A place within myself so I can be at ease
A place where I'm not alone
Recovering from my mistakes making myself strong
Building my strength which had gotten weak
So when I stand up I'll be at my peak
Able to touch things I once couldn't grab
I can see clearly now
This is a promise of God I know I can have
I'm sharing my story so all can be winners
Jesus died for all known as sinners
Because he and I both know it can't be done alone
That's why he's close by waiting to answer the phone
To speak a solution to whatever problem one may have
To help you see better your journey destination or path
Then one will see that place of peace I'm talking about
Knowing God's there to intervene in all your bouts

GODLY PEACE AND LOVE

This couple here goes good with the heart like hand and glove
They will make you feel so warm even when it's cold
Being protected by God standing up bold
For who you really are and what you proclaim
This peace here is more than fortune and fame
You'll be in the spotlight for the whole world to see
Not for who you were but what you came to be
An inspiration for others traveling down your old path
I gave it up for life you do the math
It's real simple for you to add
I found better and left behind bad
You too can do the same
Just do a self-inventory that's the one to blame
Now the door can open for God to really come in
He'll make that peace flow within
It will flow in you with much clout
You'll have a glow about you brighter than the sun when it comes out

IN YOU LORD

In you lord I put my trust let me not be put to shame
I know it's not all my fault but everyone's trying to blame
Not just for my wrongs but theirs too
When the truth is found many will know they are heirs too
With you and joint heirs with your son
Surrounded by blessings waiting on someone to come
Not pointing fingers because one doesn't have a clue
If you count them the majority comes back to you
That's why I put my faith and trust above
Because I'm constantly showered with nothing but love
So I can learn to love back in a special way
No matter the circumstance season or day
So in you lord I put my trust knowing I won't be put to shame
Because I can hear you day by day calling my name

THANK YOU LORD

Thank you lord for who you are
Helping your children that walk in the dark
Trying to bring them out to see that they're just like me
Not nearly perfect and make mistakes
Focusing on differences leaves more room for
aches you hold my hand leading the way
Forgiving my wrongs day by day
Showing me how to turn them around
Back to life no longer suppressed down
Seeing myself for who I really am
Child of the living God known as the "Great I AM"
So I thank you lord for making me simple and knowing the truth
Because complication will have you blind without a clue

Beginning and End

It's time to rise to the calling bestowed upon you
To give honor and glory to the one who created you
The one who took nothing and turned it into his master plan
Leading you out of bondage holding your hand
Telling you don't look back
Leave your past where it belongs behind your back
Stay looking forward toward your future
Everyone needs to be taught and he's the tutor
He'll teach you the way to go
Still holding your hand because you've been chose
To do a job for him and not yourself
To show others who are blind or maybe even death
Those that can't see or hear the truth
They will start to see him for him and you'll be the proof
His love for you is like a mother holding her newborn lightly
He's precious too but his name is God Almighty

Who am I

I'm that man searching for the true meaning of love
Where do I find it here on earth or somewhere else
This was a feeling I couldn't find by myself
I'm that man who took what was so easy and made it real hard
Like pulling the wrong number when there's only one card
I'm the one who hid in the darkness for so long
Waiting for the light to show me my wrong
I'm the one who tossed and turned in his sleep at night
Knowing there's a blessing in my sight
I'm that man who thought he was never loved
Constantly searching for peace from up above
I'm that man who must put up a good fight
Even when things just don't seem right
When you're ready you'll get to see who you really are
You'll see the big picture when you open up your heart
So the real question and answer is not who I am but who you are
I realize now I didn't have to look very far
I'm the one God sent his son for so I wouldn't have to worry
anymore
I'm glad I didn't faint or give up
Now I have what he calls a full cup
When the pieces came together it seemed so odd
I see why because who I really am is a child of God

ILLUSTRATION FOR WHO AM I

Not knowing who you really are besides a vessel with attachments can put an individual in a bind. One may wander looking for answers. In my case I looked in inappropriate places. People, places, and things won't define who you are. If one is not careful these can and will lessen you're chances of finding the true essence of yourself. These were lessons I had to learn. I must have stayed strong through all that I've encountered. Here I am sharing my story with the hopes of making someone's light brighter or turning it on. Through all my adversities I didn't get the opportunity to know myself. It took for me to run into many brick walls to find restoration of my sanity. I came to believe in a power greater than myself and stood willingly for it to operate. My perplexed moments were allowed to happen so I could find out who I am. My answers were found to who I am within myself. My friend I'm a child of God. Let no one take that right away from you and watch how far God/Jesus takes you.

A NEW CREATION

Now you know its possible to weather the storm
Keep moving forward because you're getting warm
Heading for the place GOD wants you to be seen
Don't worry about what's in back of you
He already wiped it clean
So you can continue excelling to higher expectations
Towards your dreams and goals because you've found motivation
You will have new strength like the days of old
Believing and knowing who you are standing up bold
Allowing nothing or no one to get in your way
It's a gift from GOD and today is your day
To receive his best because now you have a clue
His gift was designed specifically for you
Grab hold of it with no hesitation
What once was old has become a new creation

The time has come to close the chapter of this book
Maybe someone will want to take a second look
At these words or maybe his or her life
If not you maybe someone close chasing after strife
You can help them understand life's rights and wrongs
The beginning to singing a brand new song
Let others know they don't have to take my old route
I already did it for them it's time to come out
From the darkness to the light
Call on Jesus he'll take over all your battles
and struggles that we call fights

To be continued...